Bibliographic information published by the German National Library:

The German National Library lists this publication in the National Bibliography; detailed bibliographic data are available on the Internet at http://dnb.dnb.de .

Imprint:

Copyright © 2013 GRIN Verlag, Open Publishing GmbH
Print and binding: Books on Demand GmbH, Norderstedt Germany
ISBN: 978-3-668-08187-1

This book at GRIN:

http://www.grin.com/en/e-book/309528/increasing-software-development-efficiency-methodologies-and-approaches

Syed Azher

Increasing Software Development Efficiency. Methodologies and Approaches

Prototyping, Agile, Structured, Rapid Application Development and End-User Approach

GRIN Publishing

GRIN - Your knowledge has value

Since its foundation in 1998, GRIN has specialized in publishing academic texts by students, college teachers and other academics as e-book and printed book. The website www.grin.com is an ideal platform for presenting term papers, final papers, scientific essays, dissertations and specialist books.

TABLE OF CONTENTS

Executive summary

The purpose of this paper is to clearly understand about the different types of software methodologies and approaches that are available for the creation and development of a new software project with an increase in the level of efficiency. This study deals with the balance that lies between the efficiency and effectiveness of the project development in large scale industries. Initially the complexity in the development of the project is discussed and then the comparison between the types of methodology and approach is presented followed by which the best approach is selected for a civil air craft project from the perspective of a project manager. In this research the different types of methods and approaches are discussed in detail and the recommendations and conclusion about the process is also suggested for the development of the project that is to be used in the air craft corporation. Further this research reviews two peer reviewed articles and compares them thereby justifying the reason for choosing a particular approach for a civil aircraft software development process. This research also tells about the personal learning that is gained through various experiments with the help of the above mentioned methods and approaches. This research details about the efforts that are needed by the organizations towards the effective implementation of large scale information system in the aircraft corporation. Finally this research predicts about how to cumulate the formulation of results received from the study and the recommendations and how to apply these practices in the economic development of large scale industries.

1.1 Introduction

According to Ambler (2002) the software methodology is an approach that acts as a frame work through many methods to develop new software. It is a process which involves creating new software, improvement of development in project and finding the exact solution to the problems and evaluating the user requirements based on some relevant information. A software design is said to be good and fully completed only if they meet the expectations and requirements of the users. The software development for large scale Information system has strengthened the engineering industry to provide projects with high quality and high efficiency. The most important factor is that the developments of information system in an industry like air Craft Corporation is a difficult one. The only solution to handle this problem is the development of some approaches and methodologies for the proper implementation of IS in large scale. Significant effort is taken in order to improve the efficiency in the development of each and every project. Information system not only relies on the application of the software but also relies largely on the user requirements. Schwaber and Beedle (2001) have mentioned that the research methodologies and approaches are dived and classified into many types. These research overviews about the different types of methodologies and approaches and their role in large scale air craft industry. The word 'methodology' generally refers to the design that is developed in the information systems. Many methods are considered in this project to find the best method and it is suggested by the software project manager for the efficient and effective development of the project and also to meet the user requirements. Abrahamsson et al (2002) has described that the development of the information system is viewed as a technical change in the IS industry. The process of these methodologies is to find the problem in earlier stage of the development process and a solution is evaluated, tested and then implemented in the project to obtain a fully completed project without any errors in it. The development approaches and methodologies are used in the IS mainly to support the definition of information system and the approaches like structured, prototyping focuses on the development of these methodologies to provide IS more effectively and efficiently. Boehm (2002) have mentioned that the first part of the research is to be done on the discussion to provide details regarding the different types of

2

software development methodologies that are used to plan, structure and improve the process of development in information system in large scale information system and then from that one method is to be suggested and the reason is justified for the choice of that software development methodology. Cockburn (2001) has described that the next part is to elaborate in detail about the different types of software development approaches that are used for the creation of new software which involves many steps and methods. Then it discusses about the choice of approach that is suggested for the improvement of the organization. For this discussion it uses different concepts of development of software methodologies like MSA, DSDM, Use case driven methodology to develop new software and different software developmental approaches like prototyping, agile, structured, end-user and RAD approaches for minimizing the risks and modification of the project during the development of the project in the information system in the air craft corporation (Larman, 2003).

1.2 An overview of software development methodologies for large scale IS projects in engineering industry

According to Beck (2005) software development methodology is referred as a frame work that is mainly used to plan, structure and improve the process of development in information system. The software methodologies can be designed in many ways. There are several methodologies used in engineering industry to improve and minimize the risks by developing new software. The creation of new software involves many steps; methods and approaches which ensures for the proper development of the project. The software development methodologies are mainly considered for the development of the project and to meet the requirements of the users. El Emam (2003) has mentioned that the problem in the information system is not based on the hardware rather it completely lies with the software. Hence solutions are found for the development of this software by taking into account about the

3

problem faced by the software during the development. Here the different concepts for the development of software methodologies like MSA, DSDM, and Use case driven methodologies are discussed and compared for the proper development of the project which are mentioned below.

1.2.1 MSA (Modern Structure Analysis) Methodology

According to Fowler and Highsmith (2001) the MSA (Modern Structure Analysis) Methodology was developed by Yourdon and states that he gives priority to people, interaction with people, skills, various talents people, and communication since it has great effects on their performance. This methodology does not describe about the phases involved in the project rather it details the activities that are less sequential. In simple words it means that every process must be fully completed before entering into the next incremental level. The process involves the control and feedback of the activities that is undergone in the process. Here surveys are done in order to find the feasibility of the project. An analysis is done in order to transfer the policy and scheme to assign various parts of specification. After the implementation of the parts the quality control of the project is tested and then implemented to check the development of the project.

1.2.2 Dynamic Systems Development Model (DSDM) Methodology

Palmer and Felsing (2002) have mentioned that the second methodology discussed is about the Dynamic Systems Development Model. This methodology was developed in 1990 by United Kingdom. The model is developed from the evolution of a practice called as the rapid application development (RAD).DSDM promotes best training and documentation for the development of agile software tools and techniques. DSDM mainly focuses on the user involvement, delivery of products at the right time, development during reversible changes, integrated testing of lifecycle and cooperation between the stake holders, iterative development of convergence and fitness for business process.

1.2.3 EM/ST-Incremental Evolutionary Methodology/Structured Techniques Prototype

According to Arisholm et al (2007) incremental Evolutionary Methodology is also an iterative approach which was developed by Callaos et al in 1992.This methodology is a process in which a series of small or mini waterfall is created and all the steps of this methodology gets completed in every step that it undergoes before entering into the next incremental step. The process is mainly done on small parts of the system software. In simple word it is defined as the process in which the project requirements are added in the process before entering into the evolutionary phase. Abrahamsson et al (2002) has mentioned that the main goal of this methodology is to develop the information system in a serialized way. When the process is under development both the product quality and the process is measured in an efficient way. An uncertainty with high cost is developed in the process. This uncertainty minimizes the project development. Entropy is created in order to arrange the prototypes and attain the project efficiently.

1.2.4 Use case (Use case driven Methodology)

According to Wendroff (2002) the Use case driven Methodology developed by Jacobson model focuses on the early detection and consists of many sub process like analysis, component, construction and tests and reduction of the projects risk. The sub processes are basically independent in nature which means that the output of one process does not disturb the other at any cost. This model is a highly sophisticated model used in large scale to find the risks in the project. The main goal of this methodology is to explore the complexity in the information software. It also aims at the development of the project by various sequence methods. It gains rapid development with the help of the Use case driven method by greatly emphasizing on the effectiveness of the project and the user analysis. This method depends upon the activities that are carried out, knowledge management and it also strengthens the methodology by maximizing the efficiency of the process. It can be used in many projects in order to reduce the risk and develop the project in such a way where both in efficient and effective manner which is the major benefit obtained from this methodology.

1.3 Justification of choice of methodology

Hence from the above Ahmed et al (2010) clearly understood that Software development methodology is used to improve the process of development in information system in various industries. All the methods mentioned above are used to develop the project in an efficient and effective manner. As a software project manager, in a civil aircraft corporation I hardly suggest that Use Case driven methodology is the best method when compared to the other three methodologies that can be used for the successful economic development of the project in the aircraft corporation, since it minimizes the risks and develop the project in both efficient and effective way and it the implementation of the process is also cheap than the other two methods that are discussed. Boehm and Turner (2003) have mentioned that the Use case driven Methodology model highly focuses on the early detection of the risks and it consists of many sub process like analysis, component, construction and tests and reduction of the projects risk. The sub processes are basically independent in nature which means that the output of one process does not disturb the other at any cost when implemented in industry like Air Craft Corporation. As a project manager I also suggest that this model is a highly sophisticated model and can be used in large aircraft corporation to find the risks in the project at earlier stage of the development because the efficiency of the product is high when compared to that of the modern structure analysis method and the dynamic system method.

6

Nikiforova, Nikulsins and Sukovskis (2009) have described that the main goal of this methodology is to explore the complexity in the information software. It can also be used for the development of the project by various sequence methods. As per my knowledge the rapid development is gained by the use case driven method since it greatly emphasizes on the effectiveness of the project and the user analysis. This method also depends on the activities that are being carried out, knowledge management and it also strengthens the methodology by maximizing the efficiency of the process. Hence as a project manager I suggest that the use case driven method is the best one to be used in the aircraft corporation in order to reduce the risk and develop the project in both efficient and effective way which is the major benefit obtained from this methodology and will lead to the success of the project development.

1.4 An overview of software development approaches for large scale IS projects in engineering industry

According to Peterson (2009) there are different types of approaches used in the information system projects to develop the software projects. Each approach acts as a framework and it helps to create and develop the software program. The main purpose of using this approach is to maintain the desired project. There are several approaches that can be used for the development of the project. Orr (2002) has described that the creation of new software involves many steps, methods and approach which ensures for the proper development of the project and it will also the person who develops the project to come up with a fully completed project without any risks in the project. Hence there are much development approaches that are used in the information system field to develop the project and minimize the risks in the process with the help of the following.

1.4.1 Prototyping Approach

Cho (2008) has mentioned that software prototyping is an iterative approach that involves in the process of creation of large number of prototypes. In this part of the process the incomplete version of the program or project is developed and but not fully completed. This process does not allow for the complete development of the project instead it handles some particular parts selected from a large project and developed traditionally. Prototypes are mainly used in engineering industry to find and control the uncertainty in the development of the project. Many industries like software and engineering industry incorporates this approach to create prototypes that is used during the implementation of the process. According to Arisholm et al (2007) has mentioned that the main goal of this approach is to encourage the application development by splitting a large project into small parts and then it develops the project. The approach is classified into two type's namely experimental approach and exploratory approach. The exploratory approach is used to find the requirement of the products and the experimental approach is used to find solutions to the problems that are found in the experimental approach. The prototyping approach refines the project frequently and helps to develop a project in such a way that it meets the expectation of the customers. Hence it is said as traditional development methodology. It reduces the risks involved in the projects by making into small pieces of segment through which the modifications can be easily done while the process is under development.

1.4.2 Agile Approach

Agile approach consists of agile method that is used for the development of the project management which was proposed by Ken Schwaber. The main aim of this methodology is to improve the productivity of the team in a heavy manner. It concentrates more on the development of the project than the process that is used for the development of the project.

The agile is characterized by the backlog of the prior work done, completion of fixed backlogs items that are large and about the planning session of backlog items that are to be defined in the process (Layman et al, 2004). The agile is facilitated by a master who acts as a buffer between the team and influences the master. The solution for the given work is delivered at a high speed to the users and it also meets the user satisfaction at regular basis. The software that is developed is regularly delivered to the market and customers. It changes according to the specifications incorporated. Both the client and the developers mingle with the people in the team easily. The agile adopts an empirical approach and focuses in increasing the ability of the team in an agile manner to solve the emerging challenges (Maurer and Martel, 2002).

1.4.3 Structured Approach

According to Vijayasarathy (2008) the structured approach is a process used for the creation of new software and also it is used to modify the software that is developed. This approach mainly uses program development cycle for the development of application software. The main goal of this approach is to define the problem and plan, build, check and modify the correct solution to the problem that occur during the development of the project. This approach uses heavy budget and take a lot of time to complete the project. In simple words it is said that this approach is time consuming and it can be completed only as a team. In the definition it is very important to understand in detail about the reason for the problem. Martin (2002) has mentioned that the next step after defining is to plan a solution to overcome the problem for that data types and algorithms are used. The next is to build in which the algorithm is transformed into code. The next step after the creation of code is to check that whether it works correctly. The final step is to modify the code and implement to the project to obtain the results to satisfy the users.

1.4.4 Rapid Applications Development Approach

Rapid Applications Development Approach is used for creating software in a sustainable environment and allows flexibility in the process of modeling. It is a sequential method that uses case tools for the development of the software. The Rapid Applications Development aims to lower the cost of the software requirements and it is used mainly in small projects. The system requirements are determined at the initiation of the process and automated tools are used to develop the software (MacCormack, 2001). It allows reuse of the code in order to develop the project at high speed. The Rapid Applications Development focuses mainly on the following factors like, usage of simple codes, reduction in cost, reduction in feedback cycle's length and testing the code whether it is good. The RAD approach is very cheap to construct and it is similar to structured approach. RAD can be used in all portions of the project to develop good software (Szalvay, 2004).

1.4.5 End-User Approach

The End-User Approach was developed by Wilson.C and it focuses on the problems involved in the project and it also develops a new program to meet the requirements of the users. This approach is used mainly in small projects since it lacks its formal stages before entering into the next level but it is very useful in case of small scale projects. This approach does not cost heavy for the development of the project. It is also useful if the requirements of the end-users are clearly known because only after the requirements of the end-users are known this approach can meet the need of the users. The final project thus obtained can be stored and used of long time or many years unless changes done in the procedure (Williams et al, 2004). The approach can be easily built and maintained only by the developer who built it. This approach can be altered at any point of time to meet the user requirements and also can be rebuilt easily. The project can be quickly developed when compared to other approaches. In

10

simple words it means that this approach is not time consuming like others. It is also available at cheap cost which is the major benefit in this approach. Documentation is not done in this approach and it is difficult to incorporate this approach in large scale. But it can be used in many small projects to reduce the risk and develop the project in both efficient and effective way at cheap cost and quickly which is the major benefit obtained from this approach (Bailey et al, 2002).

1.5 Justification of the choice of software development approach

Therefore from the above mentioned approaches it is clear that Software development approach is used in the development of process for creating new software solutions or modifying the existing software solutions. It is also used to improve the process of development in information system in various industries. As a software project manager, in a civil aircraft corporation I strongly suggest that Agile Approach is the best method that can be used in an industry like air Craft Corporation for the success and development of economic strategies (DeMarco and Boehm, 2002). The main aim of Agile Approach is to improve the productivity of the team in a heavy manner. Apart from this it also aims at the development of the system than the process involved in the development. The agile is characterized by the backlog of the prior work done, completion of fixed backlogs items that are large and about the planning session of backlog items that are to be defined in the process. The agile is facilitated by a master who acts as a buffer between the team and influences the master. The solution for the given work is delivered at a high speed to the users. It changes according to the specifications incorporated in the process. Both the client and the developers mingle with the people in the team easily. The agile adopts an empirical approach and focuses in increasing the ability of the team in an agile manner to solve the emerging challenges (Turk, France and Rumpe, 2002). According to Williams and Cockburn (2003) the agile approach is

11

suggested because it delivers the project quickly to the clients and in the market but the other approaches that are discussed does not act that smartly as agile does. More over the project is delivered to the clients on regular basis without any fail which is not applicable in other approaches since it sometimes forgets to deliver the project at right time to the users. Many industries adapt this technique mainly for the proper delivery of the project since it is the main thing that is to be considered in the development of a project. As a project manager I also suggest that the software that is developed is regularly delivered to the market and users. Therefore in a company like air craft corporation it is necessary to adapt such approach since the work is completed quickly and delivered promptly without any delay to the users (Poppendieck and Poppendieck, 2003).

1.6   Review of peer reviewed articles on software development

The Strategic approach on the study of project management in large scale development with dynamics of system management is done in order to clearly understand about the process of software development project that is implemented in the agile approach (Glaiel, 2012). This article tells us about the plan, execution and monitoring of the software development project with the help of following approaches like waterfall, plan driven approach and heavy weight approach. It also provides information regarding the schedules that takes long development for the completion of the project using the agile development method and regarding the failure, pressure that is scheduled, defects, changes in requirements, project delay and increase in cost that occur due to the rapid changes in the environment. Many industries would have suffered from this problem but by incorporating agile software development it can be easily solved since this approach has high flexibility and it works efficiently in the development of the project. This article also discusses about the implementation of the agile software methods as a team. It also predicts the transformation of agile software development into de-facto method in the engineering field for the process development and at present it has entered into IT field and other fields like defense and aero space. The agile process development method discussed in this research clearly depicts the impacts that are provided by the agile practices in the development of good software. Here different management approaches and six experiments along with the sub parameters are elaborated and compared with the agile development method and distinguished based on their performances. Finally this article predicts about how to cumulate the formulation of results received from the study and the recommendations the method to apply these practices in the economic development of the large scale software development industry.

The second article discussed is regarding the comparison between the three information system methodologies in relation with the efficiency and effectiveness of the project. This article has faced many crises during the development of new software. It shows about the strengthening of methods that are used for the development of the software to provide high quality of products with increase in both efficiency and effectiveness. It also details about the various aspects that influences the crisis to a large extent (Rojaz, Perez and Bolivar, n.d.,). These aspects are also taken into consideration in order to balance the effectiveness and efficiency in the project development. The primary purpose of this article describes the three methodologies and are elaborated based on their different concepts and to find which method supports efficiently and effectively well for the development of the information system in large scale. Initially it describes about the background that leads for the proliferation of complexity in the development of the project in large scale IS industry and then it is followed by the comparison between the effectiveness and efficiency in the development of the IS. Three methodologies with different types of concepts are studied here. First is the MSA (Modern Structure Analysis) Methodology which was developed by Yourdon which tells about the feasibility in the development of the project. Second is the IEM/ST-Incremental Evolutionary Methodology/Structured Techniques Prototype developed by Callaos et al in 1992 which details about the development of information system in a serialized way and the product quality and the process of development is measured in an efficient way. Third is the Use case driven Methodology developed by Jacobson which focuses on the early detection and consists of many sub process like analysis, component, construction and tests and reduction of the projects risk. This article finally provides information regarding the efforts that are taken to produce effective development project and not taking into account about the concepts.

1.7   Comparison of the reviewed articles and their contribution towards software development

Hence from the above mentioned peer reviewed articles on software development it is clearly understood that the second article discussed on the comparison between the three information systems methodologies in relation with the efficiency and effectiveness of the project is used to improve the process of the development in information system in various industries. The three methodologies with different types of concepts studied here are namely MSA (Modern Structure Analysis) Methodology, the IEM/ST-Incremental Evolutionary Methodology/Structured Techniques Prototype, Use case driven Methodology developed. This article shows about the strengthening of methods that are used for the development of the software to provide high quality of products with increase in both efficiency and effectiveness. It also details about the various aspects that influences the crisis to a large extent (Rojaz, Perez and Bolivar, n.d.,). It also elaborates about the background that leads for the proliferation of complexity in the development of the project in large scale IS industry and then it is followed by the comparison between the effectiveness and efficiency in the development of the IS. This article finally provides information regarding the efforts that are taken to produce effective development project and not taking into account about the concepts. Therefore as a project manager I suggest that the second peer reviewed article is the best one to be used in the aircraft corporation in order to reduce the risk and develop the project in both efficient and effective way which will lead to the success of the software project development.

1.8 Conclusion

This research evaluates about the different types of approaches and methodologies that are selected and compared with the already available information system methods and the best method is chosen and suggested by the Project manager of the organization for the economic development and improvement of the aircraft corporation. The major reason for the selection of software development methods and approaches is to control the development of process and the selection is done by based on the problem of the project. The first part of the research provides the discussion regarding the different types of software development methodologies that improves the process of development in information system in large scale information system. The next part elaborates in detail about the different types of software development approaches that are used for the creation of new software which involves many steps and methods. The results obtained from the research indicate that the approaches and methodologies form a coherent part in the development of the information system in large scale. Each presents a different view with some similar connections among themselves that are apparent. Thus the above mentioned types of software development methodologies and approaches indicate an academic discipline the formation of the information systems in an organization. Thus the comparison of the IS puts forth the various software method and approach that can be used for the development of process and also for the economic development in the air craft corporation.

Now a days the software methodologies and approaches focus mainly on two things that are very important for the economic development of the organization. That is the type of software development methodology and approach and the type of documentation done which produces best results in the development of information system. The development is also based upon the experience that is obtained from the research in large scale. The principle of the research that is presented is the most important task that is to be considered. After the completion of this research as a project manager I conclude that in the development of software project it is important that each team must be different from one another and must choose the best methodology and approach according to the needs of the users.

References

- Abrahamsson, P., Salo, O., Ronkainen, J and Warsta, J (2002), *Agile Software Development Methods: Review and Analysis.* VTT Publications, New Delhi.

- Abrahamsson, Pekka, Salo and Outi (2002), *Agile Software Development Methods*, VTT Publications, New Delhi, pp 39.

- Ahmed A, Ahmad S, Ehsan N, Mirza E and Sarwar S Z (2010),"*Agile Software Development: Impact on Productivity and Qulaity*", in the Proceedings of IEEE ICMIT, UK.

- Ambler S W (2002), *Agile Modeling*, John Wiley and Sons, New York.

- Arisholm E, Gallis H E, Dybå, T., Sjøberg, D (2007), "*Evaluating Pair Programming with Respect to System Complexity and Programmer Expertise*", IEEE Transactions in Software Engineering, 33(2), pp. 65-86.

- Arisholm E, Gallis, H.E., Dybå, T and Sjøberg, D (2007), "*Evaluating Pair Programming with Respect to System Complexity and Programmer Expertise*", IEEE Transactions in Software Engineering, 33(2), pp. 65-86.

- Bailey P, Ashworth N and Wallace N (2002), "*Challenges for stakeholders in adopting XP*", in: Proc. 3rd International Conference on eXtreme Programming and Agile Processes in Software Engineering—XP2002, pp. 86–89.

- Beck K (2005), *Extreme Programming Explained: Embrace Change*, Second ed. Reading, Mass.: Addison-Wesley, New York.

- Boehm B (2002), "*Get Ready for Agile Methods, with Care,*" IEEE Computer, vol. 35, no. 1, pp. 64-69.

- Boehm B and Turner R (2003), "*Balancing Agility and Discipline: A Guide for the Perplexed*, Addison, Wesley, UK.

- Cockburn A (2001), *Agile Software Development. Reading*, Addison Wesley Longman, Massachusetts.

- Cho, J (2008), *Issues and Challenges of agile software development with SCRUM.* Issues in Information System, VOL IX, No. 2.

- DeMarco T and Boehm B (2002), *"The agile methods fray"*, IEEE Computer, UK, pp 90–92.

- El Emam K (2003), *"Finding Success in Small Software Projects,"* Agile Project Management, vol. 4, no. 11.

- Fowler M and Highsmith J (2001), *"The Agile Manifesto,"* in Software Development, pp. 28-32.

- Glaeil F (2012), *Agile Project Dynamics: A Strategic Project Management Approach to the Study of Large-Scale Software Development Using System Dynamics*, Working Paper CISL# 2012-05, loan School of Management, MIT, accessed 10 October 2013, http://web.mit.edu/smadnick/www/wp/CISL- Sloan%20WP%20spreadsheet.htm.

- Larman C (2003), *"Iterative and Incremental Development: A Brief History,"* IEEE Computer, New York.

- Larman C and Basili V (2003), *"A History of Iterative and Incremental Development,"* IEEE Computer, vol. 36, no. 6, pp. 47-56.

- Layman L, Williams L and Cunningham L (2004), *"Motivations and Measurements in an Agile Case Study"*, Proceedings of ACM SIGSOFT Foundation in Software Engineering Workshop Quantitative Techniques for Software Agile Processes (QTE-SWAP), Newport Beach, CA.

- Lehman T J and Sharma A (2011), *"Software Development as a service: Agile Experiences"*, in annual SRII Global Conference, UK.

- MacCormack, A (2001), *Product-development practices that work: How Internet companies build software.* MIT Sloan Management Review (Winter, pp 75–84.

- Martin, R C (2002), *Agile Software Development, Principles, Patterns and Practice*, Prentice Hall, New York.

- Maurer F and Martel S (2002), *"Extreme Programming: Rapid Development for Web-Based Applications"*, IEEE Internet Computing, 6(1), pp. 86-91.

- Nikiforova, O., Nikulsins, V and Sukovskis, U (2009), *Integration of MDA Framework into the Model of Traditional Software Development*. In: Frontiers in Artificial Intelligence and Applications, Databases and Information Systems V, vol. 187, pp. 229–239. IOS Press, Amsterdam.

- Orr, K (2002), CMM versus *Agile Development: Religious Wars and Software Development*. Agile Project Management Executive Report 3, 7, Cutter Consortium, Arlington, MA.

- Palmer S R and Felsing J M (2002), *A Practical Guide to Feature-Driven Development*. Upper Saddle River, Prentice Hall PTR, New York.

- Peterson, K (2009), *A Comparison of Issues and Advantages in Agile and Incremental Development between State of the Art and an Industrial Case, Journal of System and Software*, USA.

- Poppendieck M and Poppendieck T (2003), *Lean Software Development*. Boston: Addison Wesley, USA.

- Rojaz T., Perez. M., Bolivar S., *A comparison of three information systems development methodologies related to effectiveness/efficiency criteria*, retrieved on 10th October 2013 from http://citeseerx.ist.psu.edu/viewdoc/summary?doi=10.1.1.133.9061

- Schwaber K and Beedle M (2001), *Agile Software Development with Agile Software Development with Scrum*, Prentice-Hall, New York.

- Szalvay V (2004), *An Introduction to Agile Software Development*, Danube Technologies Inc, USA.

- Turk, France D and Rumpe R (2002), *Limitations of Agile Software Processes*; Turk, Dan France, Robert Rumpe; Colorado State University, Fort Collins, Colorado, pp 43.

- Vijayasarathy L R (2008), *Agile Software Development: A survey of early adopters. Journal of Information Technology Management* Volume XIX, Number 2.

- Wendroff P (2002), *An Essential Distinction of Agile Software Development Processes Based on Systems Thinking in Software Engineering Management*, XP 2002 Extreme Programming; pp 218.

- Williams L, Krebs W, Layman L, Antón A and Abrahamsson P (2004), *"Toward a Framework for Evaluating Extreme Programming"*, Proceedings of Empirical Assessment in Software Eng. (EASE) 2004, Edinburgh, Scot., pp. 11-20.

- Williams L and Cockburn A (2003), *"Special Issue on Agile Methods,"* IEEE Computer, vol. 36, no. 3.